# The HEART of the Concerto

### 9 Intermediate to Late Intermediate Arrangements of Themes from Great Piano Concertos

## KENON D. RENFROW

The piano concerto, a work for orchestra that highlights the piano as a solo instrument, is among the greatest compositional genres. Although orchestral works that highlight a keyboard instrument appeared as early as the Baroque period, Mozart highly refined the form in the Classical period. Several other composers, among them Haydn, Beethoven, Rachmaninoff, Schumann and Tchaikovsky, also composed monumental concertos.

The pieces in *The Heart of the Concerto* are arrangements of themes from some of these great works. While they stand alone as piano solos, they also can be performed with the accompanying orchestrations available in General MIDI format. Each example on the General MIDI disk is identified by an icon followed by the track number. Now the intermediate pianist can experience the excitement and beauty of performing these works with orchestral accompaniment.

*Kenon D. Renfrow*

# Concerto No. 4

**Themes from the 3rd Movement**

Franz Joseph Haydn (1732–1809)
Hob. XVIII/4
Arr. by Kenon D. Renfrow

# Concerto No. 11

**Theme from the 3rd Movement**

Franz Joseph Haydn (1732–1809)
Hob. XVIII/11
Arr. by Kenon D. Renfrow

# Concerto No. 21

**Theme from the 2nd Movement**

Wolfgang Amadeus Mozart (1756–1791)
K. 467
Arr. by Kenon D. Renfrow

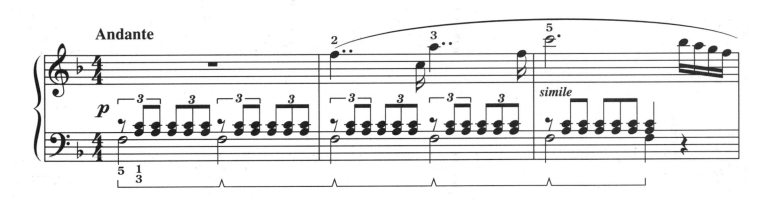

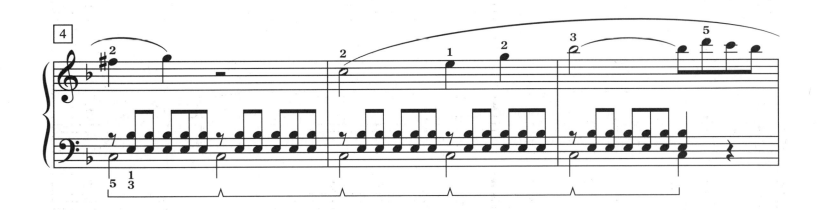

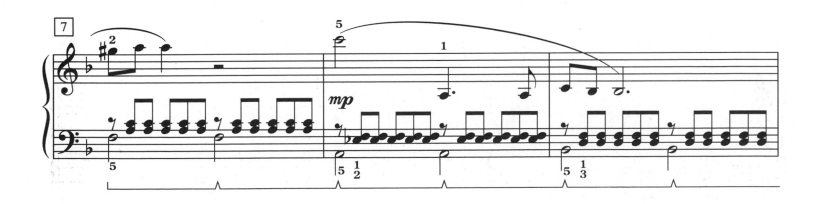

# Concerto No. 1

**Themes from the 1st Movement**

Ludwig van Beethoven (1770–1827)
Op. 15
Arr. by Kenon D. Renfrow

# Concerto No. 3

**Themes from the 1st Movement**

Ludwig van Beethoven (1770–1827)
Op. 37
Arr. by Kenon D. Renfrow

**Allegro con brio**

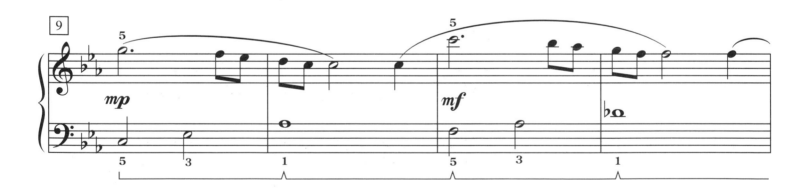

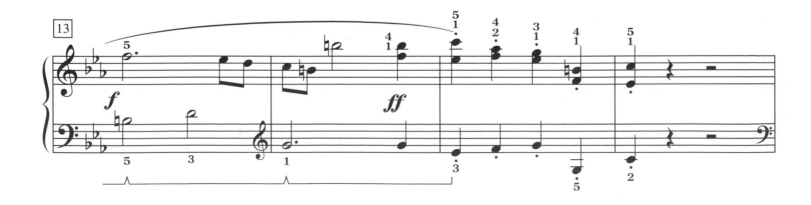

# Concerto in A Minor

**Themes from the 1st Movement**

Robert Schumann (1810–1856)
Op. 54
Arr. by Kenon D. Renfrow

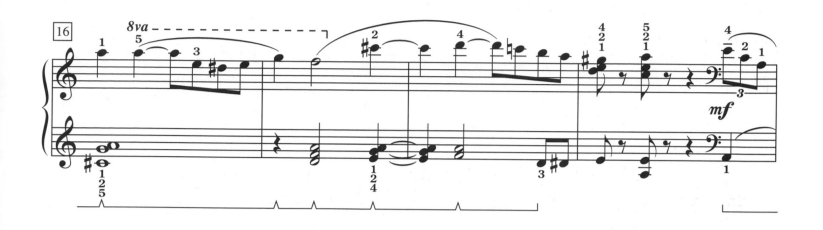

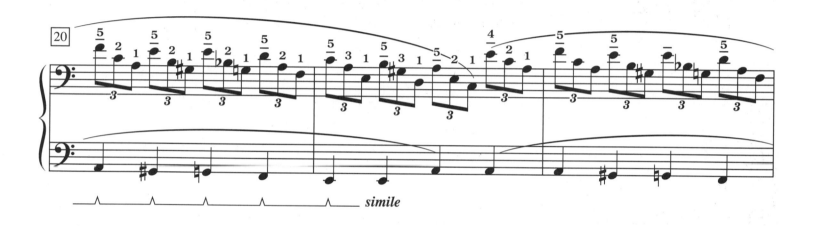

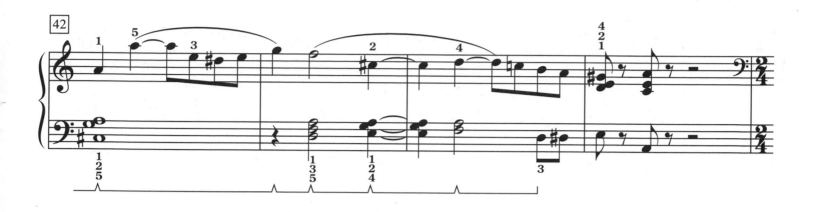

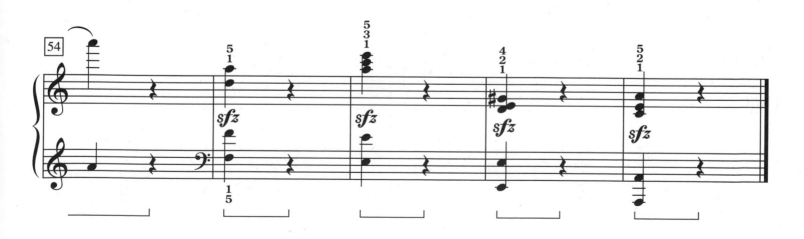

# Concerto No. 1

**Themes from the 1st Movement**

Peter Ilyich Tchaikovsky (1840–1893)
Op. 23
Arr. by Kenon D. Renfrow

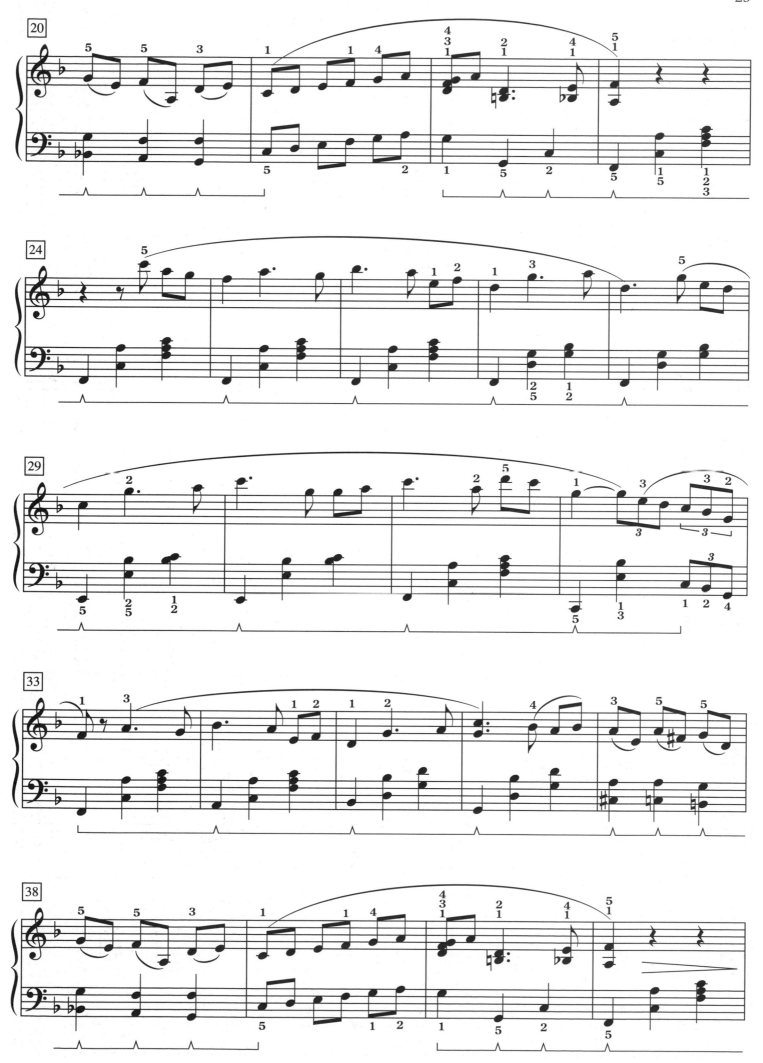

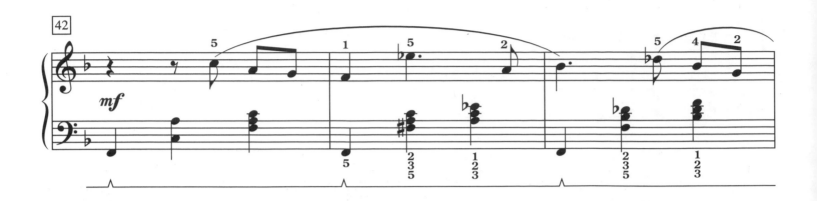

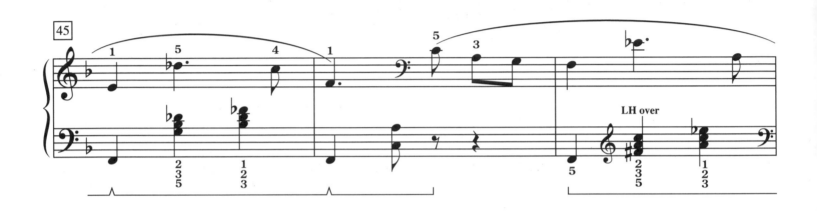

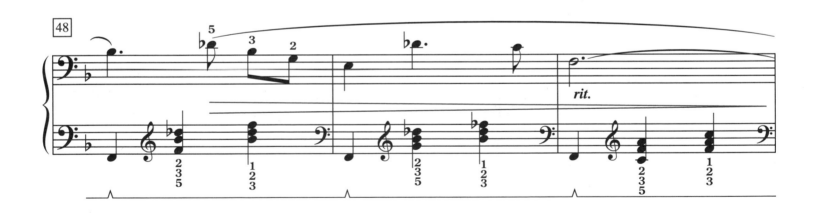

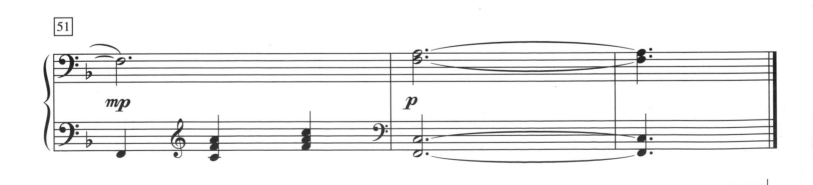

# Concerto No. 2

**Themes from the 1st Movement**

Sergei Rachmaninoff (1873–1943)
Op. 18
Arr. by Kenon D. Renfrow

# Concerto No. 2

**Theme from the 3rd Movement**

Sergei Rachmaninoff (1873–1943)
Op. 18
Arr. by Kenon D. Renfrow

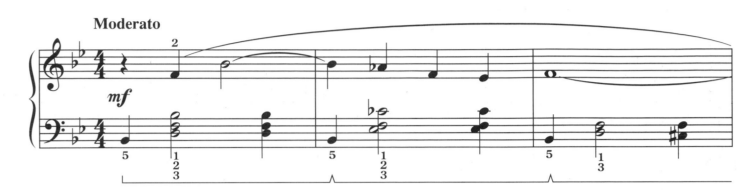

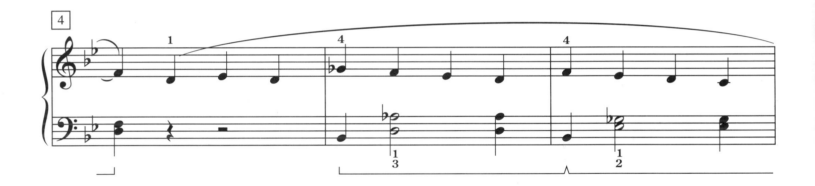

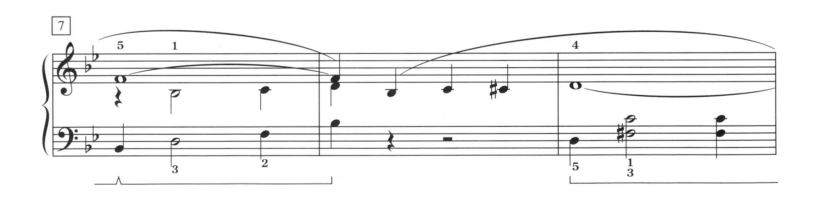

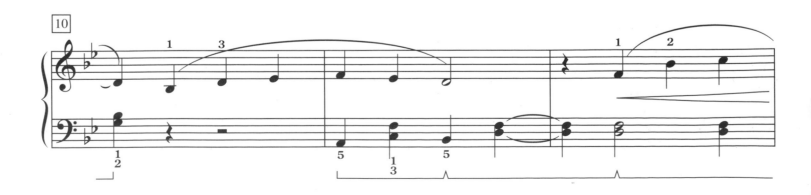

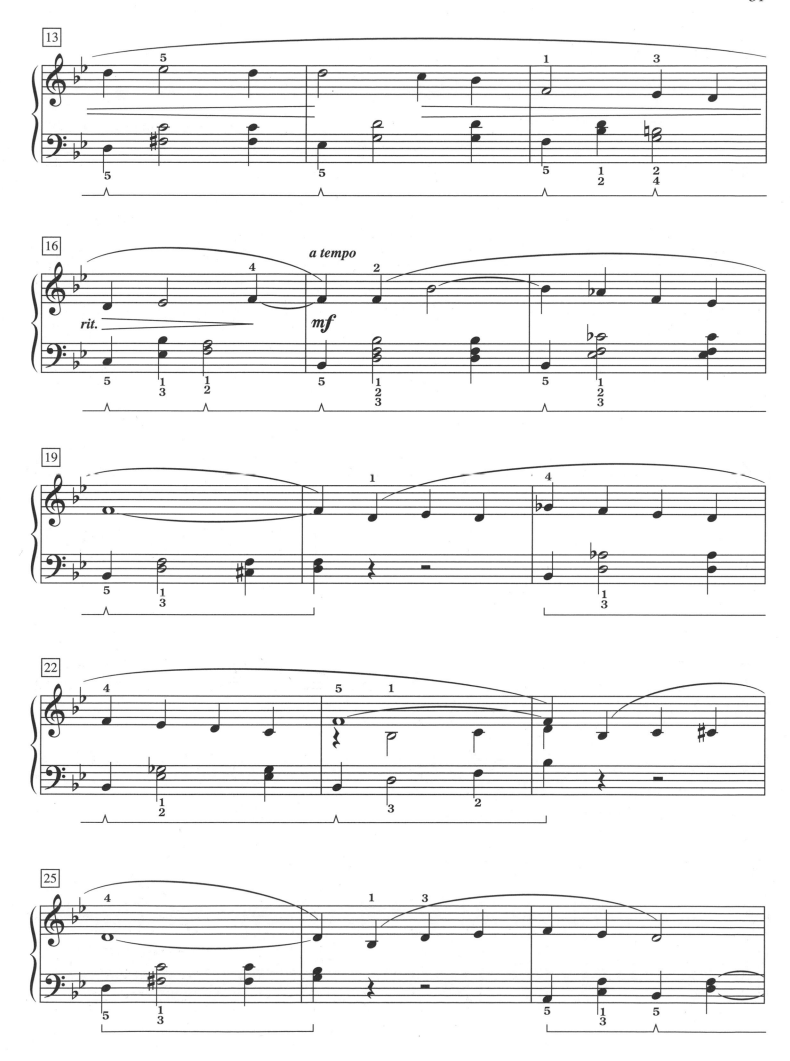